Ladki Hoon, Lad Sakti Hoon

Because Silence Was Never Our Mother Tongue

Zyrah Ashraf

BookLeaf Publishing

India | USA | UK

Made with ❤ on the BookLeaf Publishing Platform
www.bookleafpub.in
www.bookleafpub.com

Dedication

This collection of poems is dedicated to my dear friends, my family, and my beloved husband. These words are not merely verses, but a tribute to the strength of women, the echoes of history, the pursuit of justice, and the unyielding power of love and resilience. Within these pages lies my heart, woven into every line, every stanza —each a testament to the journey we share and the stories we continue to tell.

Preface

In the quiet spaces between words, there are stories that often go untold—stories of strength, of struggle, of love, and of survival. These poems are born from those spaces. Through these lines, I seek to give voice to the silences, to the forgotten narratives, to the battles fought and the victories won, no matter how small.

These poems are not just mine; they are a collective tapestry woven from the threads of defiance that runs through us all. They are for the women who have dared to stand up, for the stories of justice that demand to be heard, for the love that binds us together, and for the strength we carry in the face of adversity. They are for the quiet rebels, the unseen fighters, the hearts that endure.

May these words offer comfort, empowerment, and understanding, as they reflect the journey of all who dare to love deeply, fight fiercely, and rise with grace.

Acknowledgements

To my incredible friends and family:
You have shown me that true strength is not only about facing adversity, but about kindness, vulnerability, and standing together. Through every challenge, you have been my steady foundation, my sounding board, and my greatest cheerleaders. Thank you for all that you do.

1. Before She Could Say No

She was 12 when they wrapped her in red silk,
called it a wedding,
called it destiny,
called it God's will
She did not know how to sign her own name yet.
Did not know how to cook rice without burning it.
Did not know why her mother's eyes were oceans
the night they told her she was leaving
but still, she went—
barefoot into a future that did not belong to her.
And the groom, twice her age,
twice her weight,
twice as entitled
but only half as human,
took her hands in his,
and she wondered if they would always feel like
shackles.

Because to be a bride before you are a woman
is to be a wound before you are a body.
To be a home for someone
before you have ever been a home for yourself.
To learn how to kneel
before you ever learned how to run.

At 14, she learned how to fold silence into her throat,
how to turn her ribs into armor,
how to breathe without making a sound.
And maybe this is why
they marry girls before they bloom—
because a flower does not ask for freedom
until it has tasted the sun.

2. Hunger for Survival

In 2014, 19 year old Saba,
A young Pakistani girl
Courageously fell in love with a man below her family's
financial status
When her father found out
He pulled out a gun and proceeded to shoot her in the
head
But I wonder if it was God who chose to preserve the
best of his creation
As by some divine power, the gun misfired, and her life
was given 2 second chances that night
Once when the bullet grazed her cheek
And the second when her father put her in a sack and
threw her body in the river
It was by the grace of God that her bag fatefully untied
that night
As she battled her way into survival

If there is anything that I have learned about being a
woman
Is that we've had to suffocate our spirit to breathe
Told the most fearless parts of us to cut themselves loose
Traded in our individuality for a worthless life in
servitude

Allowing ourselves to be prey for so long
That our cries will only ever be met with blood
Our existence will only ever be met with extinction
But I wonder
if they know the kind of superpower It takes just to be
woman
to bring life into this world
The way she can meticulously create beauty through her
Its funny to assume that she would be anything less than
holy
That she would be anything less than magic
That her ability to produce is anything short of miracle
And yet why is it that I have watched men treat women
as if they were nothing more than target practice

You see
Honor is an interesting concept where I'm from
To be a woman is to be a chameleon in your own skin
It means adapting to a word that is constantly evolving
in the hands of men
It means that camouflage has been our only toolkit for
survival
So we bury our calls for freedom in the dirt
Zip tie our tongues so that they cannot cry
As we hang our sorrows out to dry
And abandon our dreams into dust
We brace our entire being to be able to hold the weight

of our family's name

As a woman the world teaches us to starve
To crave an existence that could not possibly be our own
Buckles our knees and prostrates
The arch in our backs into submission
Isn't it funny
How hungry your patriarchy is
The way wolves only learn to devour their prey
Meticulously hunting
Satiating
Savoring
When will you realize
That your existence cannot be without out survival
After all, how will you eat?

3. Fluent in Fire

I'm still learning how to speak my mother's tongue,
I'm often lost in words I should be fluent in,
And silent when the story of my people needs to be told.
I was born into a country that rises from the ashes
And I've been standing tall ever since.

4. Ruksathi - Thread by Thread

I turned to my mother,
her eyes heavy with the kind of love that speaks fluently
in sacrifice,
the kind that makes a home out of exhaustion
but never complains about the rent.

She had spent years holding herself together
so I could learn how to stand,
stitched her love into lullabies,
her dreams into the hem of my childhood,
never once asking for them back.

Her love was the kind of fire
that warmed without ever demanding to be seen,
a lighthouse that never needed applause,
just the quiet knowing that I made it safely to shore.

And as I stood there,
wrapped in a dress that was equal parts fabric and
farewell,
I realized—
every thread was a verse of her story,
woven into mine.

She had sewn my future into the seams,
stitched herself into every fold,
left pieces of her heartbeat
between the lace and the letting go.
And as I walked away,
I wasn't just wearing a gown—
I was draped in her love,
carrying her strength,
wrapped in the weight of a thousand whispered prayers,
each one unraveling behind me
like a path back home.

5. For Me, For Only Me

The first time I made chai for myself—
not for a guest,
not for the man who never thought to ask how I took
mine,
but for me, and only me—
it felt like teaching my hands a dialect
they had long forgotten how to speak

I let the water hum before it boiled,
let the cardamom break open like a secret,
let the tea leaves unfurl like they had been waiting
for this moment their whole lives.
I stood there, barefoot in a kitchen
watching steam rise like a prayer
that did not belong to anyone else.

And maybe this is what love looks like—
The quiet revolution of choosing yourself
when no one is watching.

6. Breaking Free

Every so often I am convinced that I am an echo in the dark;
My voice a distant compass always bringing me back to the direction of home.
On silent nights, I wonder what it means to be so full of dreams,
that hope becomes armor and ambition becomes steel.
I tell myself that I am all lock and key,
but if convinced,
I could create a sword out of secrets.
On warm, sunny days,
I remind myself that my heart is a thunderous ocean -
its tumultuous waves pounding against its chambers,
reminding the body it is okay to be abundant with life.
To be so full that we allow ourselves to break free into the sea;
a funneling black hole of memories, of existence, of life.

7. Sujood

Today, while reading dua after the Maghreb salah we just
finished together,
I see the smallest, oval shaped dent plastered right in the
center of Baba's fore-head.
Its rugged edges and slight discoloration
beg to answer the many nights he spent in submission,
His head bellowed to the floor as I think of the years of
sujood-
of cold floors pressed against welcoming foreheads,
and the bending of backs to the only being I've ever
known as holy: Allah.
I wonder if we know the kind of vulnerability it takes to
come flaws and all in the face of The Creator;
The way our hearts are ripped open ,
exposing the truth of our existence.
It is in the bending of the arms and knees, that I watch
my father place his dying servitude,
and I think-how beautiful is to be here,
 in this world God created "to be"
—to serve him and only him.

8. Armor Beneath the River's Flow

Ive come to learn that the world is often a room too full of its own voice.
On cold, winter morning drives I wonder what it means to live in a place where love is a language no one takes the time to translate.

I tell myself I am all open hand and hollow spaces
But if pressed I could turn my ribs into armor.
I remind myself that a heart can be all river;
rushing forward even as the world forgets to cup its hands and drink

To exist here is to hold onto softness while everything else sharpens itself into survival.
To give, even when the world is only learning how to take.

9. Poetry

I often forget that there is poetry all around me;
I hear it in the heaviness of my father's voice
every-time he calls me "beta."
I see it in the courage my mother uses every-time she
broken english's her way to getting things done
—if there was ever a metaphor for powerhouse, by god it
is her.
I see imagery in the tear that falls like the last raindrop
from a cloudy sky;
I swear the world chooses to cry with us on the days our
hearts feel the most heavy.
Poetry isn't always in rhyme,
it is in rhythm
The beating of one's heart,
the sound of one's laughter,
the furrowed eyebrows of a grumpy frown—
it is in the soul;
the way an entire being can come to life the minute you
decide to give it meaning.

10. Shalwar Kameez: The Art of Wearing Time

The paisleys dance like lost Mughal gardens,
blooming across my sleeves,
tiny echoes of emperors who once draped themselves
in tapestries of the same gold and indigo.
The threadwork whispers of caravan trails,
of spices spilling like poetry in the wind,
of hands darkened by dye,
bringing color to the world
before the world ever knew how to name it.

My grandmother's hands knew these stitches,
her fingers moving like a prayer,
pulling needle through cotton
one loop at a time.
She told me the fabric remembers—
every pull, every knot, every cut,
holds the weight of a thousand years,
of stories too stubborn to be forgotten.

I wear centuries on my skin.
I wear the echoes of bazaars bustling with barter,
the hush of looms singing in hidden courtyards,
the patience of hands that never rushed the art.

This is architecture built in silk,
a skyline of stitches, a fortress of tradition,
a rebellion against time itself.
A reminder that history is not always written—
sometimes, it is worn.

11. Zainab

Zainab, you were more than a name whispered
in the tremor of the nation's guilty breath.
You were the fire beneath the ashes,
the silent cry that burned through walls.

They never knew how to hear you,
how to feel the weight of your absence
before it was carved into history's most painful verse.
Your eyes, still innocent,
saw the world through a lens too pure
for the hands that shaped it—
hands that never stopped long enough to hold you.

You, a child, too soft for their cruel calculation,
too whole for a world so broken,
and they tore you apart

They say you are gone,
but your spirit haunts the spaces
where justice should have been,
Your story is not a footnote
but a chapter etched in every mother's heart,
every sister's silence,
every daughter's prayer.

You are not gone,
you are the language that rises
whenever we say "enough."
You are the question we cannot silence,
the future we will demand,
the future we will never stop fighting for—
where innocence is never preyed upon,
where justice is not a whisper,
but the roar of a generation
tired of being too quiet.

12. Fajr

Fajr mornings are for the quiet soul,
for those who have learned to listen
to the quiet pulse of faith.

The rhythm of the call to prayer
fills the space between thoughts,
like the softest echo of a dream
you didn't know you were having
until you woke up in the middle of it.

13. Fair and Lovely

They tell us we're **"Fair and Lovely,"**
as if the color of our skin
is a currency to be spent,
as if we should trade our melanin
for something more marketable,
more "acceptable,"
less "earthbound."

But what is fair,
if not a mirror held up to the light
that burns itself out in the process?
And what is lovely,
if not a word
we've been taught to choke on.

I wonder if the moon ever looks at the sun
and thinks,
"I wish I was a little brighter."
Does the ocean ever envy the sky,
its vastness diluted by clouds,
its waves never quite clear enough
to show their true depth?

We are not meant to fit into their idea

of what beauty should look like—
a shade, a hue,
a fleeting trend that shifts
with every season.
Our skin is not a paint swatch
to be rubbed out and replaced.
It is a tapestry woven by time,
stamped with the stories of ancestors
who walked barefoot through the same earth,
whose blood pulses through our veins
and whispers, "You are already enough."

14. Bitch Heart

I have a raging heart. A bitch of a heart that can't help but become an explosion. Her rumble is *too loud, too violent:* has too much *hand clapping, too much fire, and too much blood that spills over everything.* Sometimes she thinks of cold after-noons, of white trees shaped by white branches; a euphoria of white wonder-land--of purity. If innocence came as an object my bitch heart knows she'd call it snow. She'd put her tongue under it and let it *relinquish all her flames.* She's a turbulent earthquake waiting to collapse the world under her feet. I know she's planning on killing me; scheming somewhere underneath all the flesh--she's plotting something. She asks me, *"baby, are you afraid of falling?"* Bitch Heart knows I'm afraid of heights.

15. Battered Heart

I wonder if people know that I have a battered heart
I got it from beating myself up all the time;
But wounds are all I've ever known
Etched into the seams of what you call a beating drum;
I wonder if my chambers echoed its beat
But no amount of heart can save someone from a lack of
self preservation.

I watched myself die the minute I stopped writing for
revolution,
The minute my smiles turned into sole muscle memory
And I stopped dancing on my two left feet like the floor
was going to fall beneath me.
When this body became nothing more than a walking
corpse
A shell of once was
I watched myself fade away into the shadows
A memory of once was sun
Perhaps never more.

16. To a Loving Husband

In your love, I am both a restless flow and a steady land,
Tethered by the pull of currents
I never knew could carry me so deep.
Yet you never let me slip beneath the surface,
Your hands, like anchors, always keeping me afloat

You make me feel as though
I am not merely a reflection in your eyes,
But a song in the quiet of your soul—
A melody you know by heart,
A rhythm that pulses in the warmth between us.

17. Ramadan

I hope that when I starve,
My stomach speaks to you in verses.
Calls upon all the days it spent
Being full
Abundant-
How it yearned for its emptiness
So that you can fill it with your mercy.
 Give me hunger,
Have my soul beg to be fed by your holy
—As my body breaks in your servitude
I hope that my tongue continues to heal by your
scripture
It is my only saving grace.

18. Target Practice

The night my little 7 year old heart heard
"you're a terrorist,"
 I realized that being a Muslim meant I would always be
used for target practice.
 My faith a bulls eye
 Your ignorance the trigger.

19. Loved you Like Math

I loved you like math
Like a concave up function that was always increasing
Derivative so I could lie tangent to your curves.
Meeting you was like
making a switch to polar coordinates
 Because complex and imaginary things are given a
magnitude and direction
And being without you was like a metric space in which
exists a cauchy sequence that does not converge.

20. Bloom

Someone told me me once
That "I feel too much"
As if they could understand the sun in my gut
The way it tries to reach the darkest parts of me
Tells this seed you call a body to keep fighting for
summer
I hope for daisies to bloom,
To remind me there is beauty in things worth growing.

www.ingramcontent.com/pod-product-compliance
Lightning Source LLC
LaVergne TN
LVHW010022200726
843495LV00015B/1891